VOLVO PENTA MD5A MARINE DIESEL ENGINE

Workshop Manual

VOLVO PENTA MD5A MARINE DIESEL ENGINE

Workshop Manual

ISBN/EAN: 9783954275052
Erscheinungsjahr: 2012
Erscheinungsort: Bremen, Deutschland

© maritimepress in Europäischer Hochschulverlag GmbH & Co. KG, Fahrenheitstr. 1, 28359 Bremen. Alle Rechte beim Verlag und bei den jeweiligen Lizenzgebern.

www.maritimepress.de | office@maritimepress.de

Bei diesem Titel handelt es sich um den Nachdruck eines historischen, lange vergriffenen Buches. Da elektronische Druckvorlagen für diese Titel nicht existieren, musste auf alte Vorlagen zurückgegriffen werden. Hieraus zwangsläufig resultierende Qualitätsverluste bitten wir zu entschuldigen.

VOLVO PENTA MD5A MARINE DIESEL ENGINE

Workshop Manual

CONTENTS

Presentation   2

Dismantling

Electrical system, thermostat housing cylinder head	3
Flywheel, fuel injector pump	4
Oil pump, transmission cover, governor	5
Lubricating oil pump, camshaft, cylinder	6
Crankshaft, cylinder liner, camshaft bearing	7

Overhauling

Lubricating oil pump, sea-water pump	7 – 9
Feed pump	9 – 11
Fuel filter, crankshaft	11
Centrifugal governor, piston	12 – 13
Valve guides, nozzle sleeve	14 – 15
Valves, valve seats, rocker mechanism, injector	15 – 16
Hand start mechanism, camshaft	17

Assembling

Cylinder liner, crankshaft	18
Cylinder, camshaft, governor	19
Lubricating oil pump, transmission cover	20
Adjustment of control rod travel, assembling flywheel cover	20 – 21
Oil sump, cylinder head, feed cover	22
Fuel filter, injector, thermostat	22
Flywheel, generator, valve adjustment	24
Checking injection angle	25
Bleeding the fuel system, electrical system	26
Wiring diagram	27
Fault-tracing system	28
Special tools	29
Technical data	30 – 33

Presentation

1. Connection for hand start
2. Fuse box
3. Thermostat housing
4. Decompression lever
5. Injector
6. Oil filler Cap, engine
7. Water drain tap, gearbox
8. Oil drain plug, gearbox
9. Water drain tap, engine
10. Oil filler, gearbox
11. Sea-water pump
12. Dipstick, gearbox
13. Fuel filter
14. Bleed screw
15. Hand pump, fuel
16. Dipstick, engine
17. Oil filter

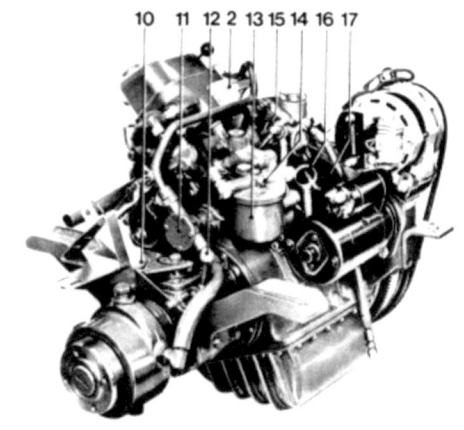

Repair instructions

Dismantling
1. Drain the cooling water and the oil from the engine. Clean externally afterwards. Loosen the water hose between the gearbox and the sea-water pump and remove the gearbox.

3. Remove the rocker cover and the fuel pipe between the pump and the injector and unscrew the rocker gear. Note! Pull the rocker gear straight up since it is centred with a guide pin 1. The other hole 2 is an oil channel.

2. Remove the generator and its drive belt, starter motor, fuel filter and fuel pump with the drain-off pipe (be careful of fuel spillage), coolant water pump with hose and thermostat housing, dipstick, temperature and oil pressure sensors. Unscrew and discard the oil filter.

4. Remove the push-rods 1, remove the cylinder head and the cylinder head gasket. Take care of the washers 2 under the nuts.

5. Remove the flywheel nuts. Spanner jaw width 55 mm (2 5/32"). Use a wooden shaft or something similar as a counter force in the flywheel spokes.

7. Remove the cover for the injection pump. Note! The bracket for the cold start is fixed with one of the screws. Take care of the spring under the cover.

6. Fit tool 884078 to the flywheel. Afterwards screw in the centre screw on the tool until the flywheel loosens.

8. Prise the lower ball joint free from the pump with a screwdriver.

9. Remove the pump screws. Position the ball in the centre and remove the pump.

11. Remove the governor by loosening the hexagonal set screw (1), the governor and the gear wheel can then be withdrawn.

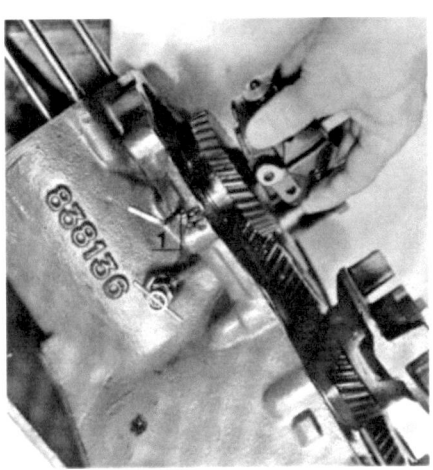

10. Remove the sump and then the transmission cover (13 screws). The lifting eye is fixed one of the screws. The cover is centralised by guide pins.

12. Remove the screw and the locking washer for the gearbox drive flange on the crankshaft and remove the flange with a puller. (Use counter force.) Remove the key afterwards.

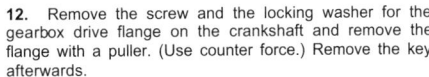

13. Remove the lubricating oil pump. Discard the gasket.

15. Remove the gearwheel on the camshaft's flywheel side (4 screws). Then remove the camshaft and the gearwheel.

14. Remove the cover (flywheel side), 10 screws. The cover is centred with guide pins. The screws by the guide pins are fitted with thick washers.

16. Mark and remove the bearing cap on the crankshaft and carefully knock out the piston through the cylinder.

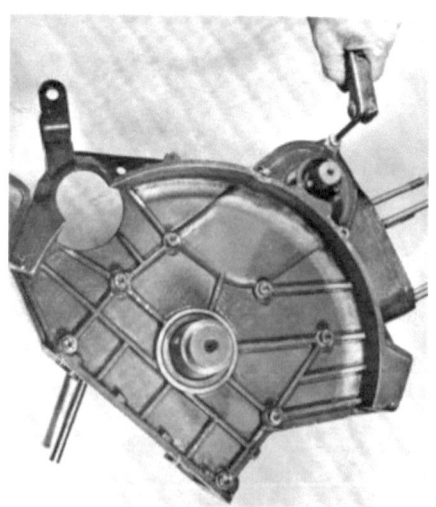

17. Remove the main bearing caps. Take care of the axial thrust bearings 1 on the transmission side. Lift the crankshaft out and the bearing shells afterwards and then the axial bearing halves.

19. Bearing replacement. Press out the camshaft bearings if they are damaged or if the wear is too great (see technical data). Clean the bearing housings and ensure that the oil channels are clean. Press in the new bearings so that the oil holes face the corresponding oil channels in the block. When the bearings are pressed in position they are to be reamed (see technical data).

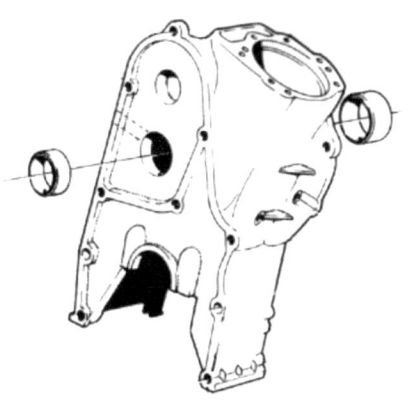

18. Mark the cylinder liner's position in the cylinder so that the same position can be obtained during assembly. Remove the cylinder liner. Use tool 884551. Use the long screw and its nut from the tool 884231 (MD21-MD32). See page 29 Special tools. Discard the 0-ring. Afterwards remove the 0-rings in the block which provide a seal for the cylinder liner and then remove the valve lifters. Wash all the parts and replace those damaged.

Oilpump
20. Remove the gearwheel's nuts and pull off the gearwheel with a puller. The gearwheel sits on a key, take care of this key.

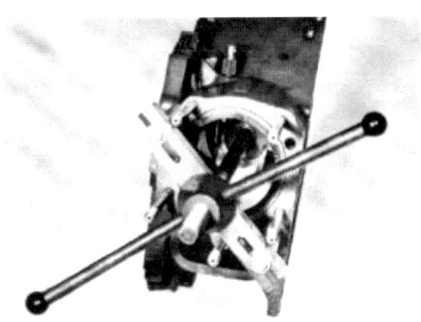

7

21. Remove the steel wire which holds the filter. Remove and clean the wire gauze thoroughly. Afterwards remove the six screws which hold the cover in position. Discard the gasket.

Overhauling the sea-water pump

23. The sea-water pump is a round flange type pump which means that it can be fitted in a position best suited to the coolant water hoses. The new pump is fitted with an 0-ring which forms a seal against the engine.

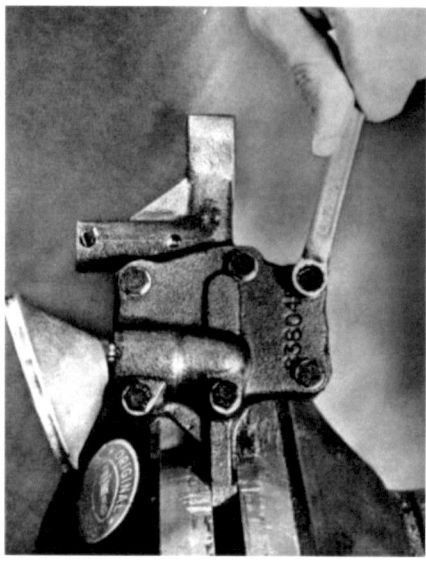

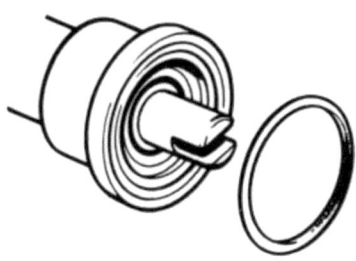

22. Remove the gearwheel from the housing. Remove the split pin for the reduction valve. Remove washer 1, spring 2 and piston 3. Clean and replace damaged parts. Assemble the lubricating oil pump in the reverse order. Note! Fit a new gasket 4 between the housing and the cover. Fix the wire mesh 5 in position with the steel wire 6 and finally lay the key in position and tighten the gearwheel 7.

24. Remove the cover (6 screws). Change the impeller with the help of two screwdrivers or something similar. Note! Protect the edges of the pump housing. See the figure. Prise out the impeller with the screwdrivers so far that the screw becomes visible.

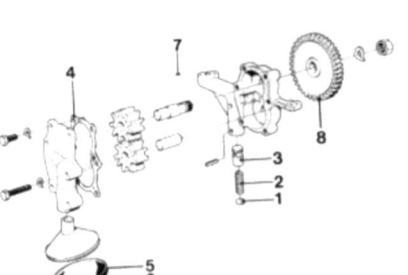

25. Unscrew the screw and withdraw the impeller from the shaft. If the sealing rings are to be replaced, the shaft and the impeller can be removed and the screw subsequently loosened.

27. Fit new sealing rings. Note! The sealing rings must face the right way, see that they do not block the drain hole in the pump housing. Smear grease on the shaft and fit it carefully in the housing. Screw it through the sealing rings so that they will not be damaged. Place the shaft so far into the housing that the hole for the screw is visible. Fit the impeller and screw in the screw. Then carefully press in the impeller so that it touches bottom. Place a new gasket on the cover and tighten the cover with the six screws.

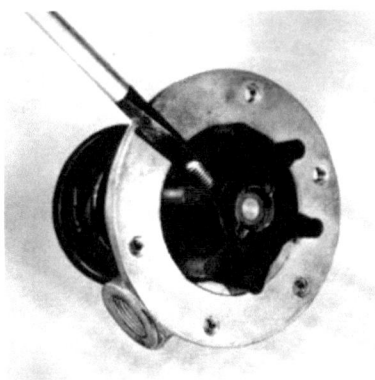

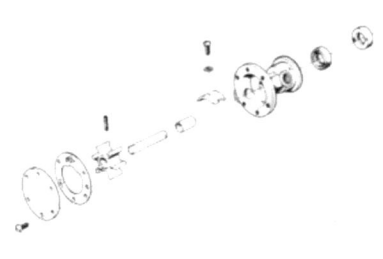

26. Remove the sealing rings 1 and the 0-ring 2 (earlier engines) and clean the housing and the shaft. (Note! The pump must be removed from the engine.) Check that there are no abrasions on the shaft. Note! A new 0-ring is not to be fitted.

Overhauling the feed pump
28. Depress the pump's lever (see fig.). If the pump "creaks" then it is sound. If it is unserviceable the diaphragm must be replaced which is done in the following manner:

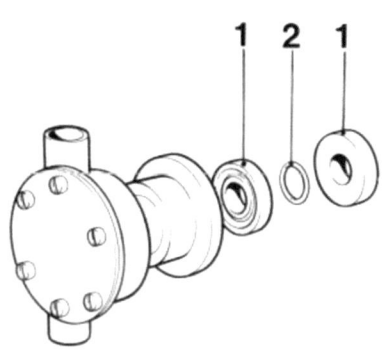

29. Remove the cover's centre screw, remove the filter 1 and clean it.

31. Depress the diaphragm and shake the pump arm spindle out until the pump arm is free. Then remove the diaphragm from the housing.

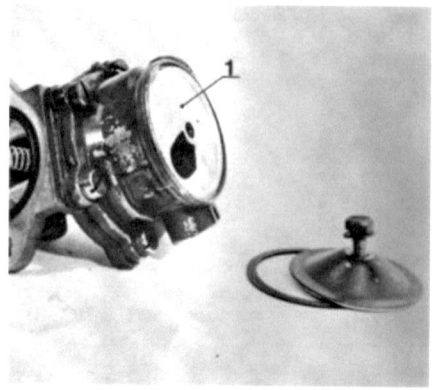

30. Remove the six screws which hold the upper and lower pump halves together. Remove the pump's spring and undo screw 2 which holds the pump arm spindle.

32. Remove screw 1 and withdraw the manual pump arm 2 and replace spring 3 if it is broken. Note! Be careful of the rubber seal which is pressed into the housing.

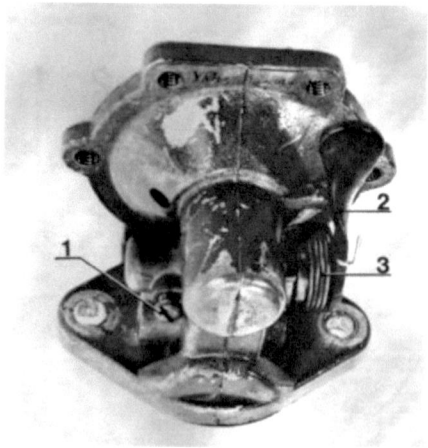

33. Clean the pump housing carefully and replace worn parts. Refit the manual pump arm. Press in the diaphragm and connect the pump arm to the diaphragm centre pin. Then push the spindle in and tighten it with the screw. Note! Do not forget the washer under the screw.
Lay the gauze filter on the upper housing and screw the cover and the gasket tight. Press in the pump arm 3, assemble the two housing halves and fit the spring retainer 2 on the mechanical pump arm 3. Note that the spring retainer can only be fitted one way. Replace the spring next and the 0-ring 4 which provides a seal for the engine.

Crankshaft
35. Remove the circlip with circlip pliers. Then remove the gear drive. Use a press or a gear puller. Clean the crankshaft and carry out control measurements of all the bearing surfaces. Grind the shaft where necessary. See technical data.

Fuel filter
34. When the filter insert is changed the centre screw 1 is removed allowing the filter holder to be removed. Afterwards remove the filter insert by lifting the plastic loop 4. Wash the filter holder clean and fit a new filter. Fit a new packing washer 5 and refit the holder to the cover with the centre screw.

36. Place the key in the crankshaft's key slot. Heat the gearwheel to approximately $100^{\circ}C$ ($212^{\circ}F$) (no more) and press it onto the crankshaft. Note! The marking on the gearwheel shall face outwards. Refit the circlip on the crankshaft.

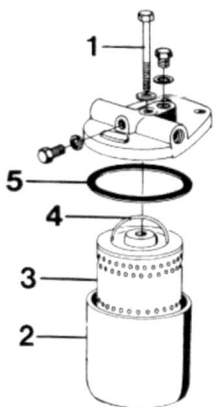

Centrifugal governor

37. Clean the governor. Check to see if the weights 2 grip on their spindle or if there is too much movement between the spindle and the governor weight. Afterwards check that the pin 1 slides easily in the spindle. Finally check both the ball bearings 3. Replace the ball bearings if they are tight. Check that all the movable parts move easily, lubricate and refit them in the reverse order.

39. Mark the piston and the connecting rod. Remove the circlips. Press out the gudgeon pin with a drift. (The piston can be heated first to ease removal.)

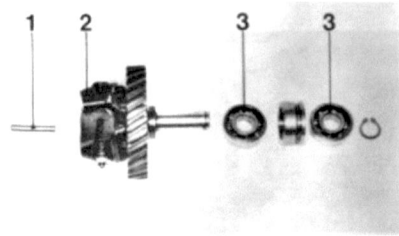

Piston

38. Remove the piston rings with the help of piston ring pliers. Clean the piston and be particularly careful about the piston ring grooves.

40. Press the bush out of the connecting rod if it is worn or damaged. Then knock out the connecting rod screws. Note! The screws must always be changed when the connecting rod has been dismantled.

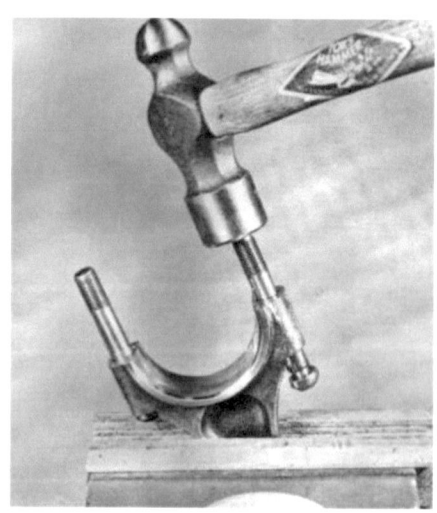

41. Knock new screws in place and press a new bush in the connecting rod. Ensure that the lubricating hole 1 in the bush aligns with the hole in the connecting rod. Ream or diamond drill the bush to an accurate free fit. Check that the gudgeon pin slides through the bush due to its own weight. (See also the technical data.) Fit one of the circlips and oil the gudgeon pin and connecting rod bush. Heat the piston to approximately $70^{0}C$ ($158^{0}F$) and assemble the piston and the connecting rod according to the marking. Note! The gudgeon pin must be able to be pressed in easily. Fit the other circlip.

43. Fit the piston rings with the help of piston ring pliers. Start with the oil scraper ring in the lowest groove. The oil scraper ring can be fitted either way. Continue with the compression ring which is marked "TOP" on one side. This marking shall face upwards when fitted. The piston ring with the chromium insert is fitted last and can be fitted either way.

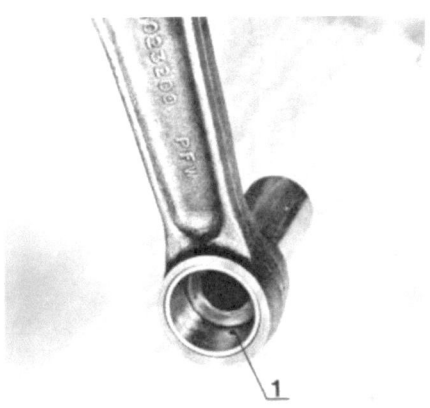

42. Control the dimensions of the piston with a micrometer. Measure at right angles to the gudgeon pin holes at the piston's lower edge. Afterwards check the new rings' play in the piston ring grooves. (See technical data.)

Cylinder head
44. Remove the collets, the collars and the valve springs with the help of a valve spring compressor. Remove the valves. Remove the valve seal from the inlet valve. Burnt valves are discarded if worn too much and damaged seats are to ne machined when necessary. (See technical data.) The valves and valve seats are to be ground together so that the mating surfaces provide a complete seal.

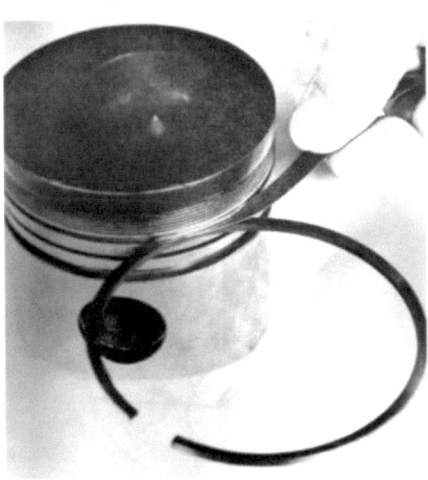

13

Replacing valve guides

45. The valve guides must be replaced if there is too much play between the valve stem and the valve guide. (See technical data.) Press out the valve guides with tool 884538.

Nozzle sleeve

47. Remove the injector sleeve with tool 884541. Insert the expanding screw in the nozzle sleeve and screw anti-clockwise until the screw has expanded and gripped the sleeve. Tighten hard so that the threads bite into the copper. Fit the yoke onto the studs which hold the nozzle. Screw on the nut and tighten until the sleeve is removed.

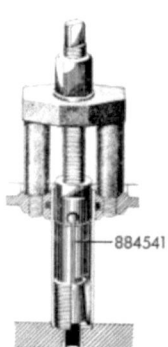

46. New valve guides are fitted with tool 884549. Use a press. This tool gives the guide the right height above the cylinder head's valve spring seat surface. Check the dimension "A" - this must be 9 mm (0,3543 in.) when the guide is pressed into place.

48. Remove the 0-ring which provides a seal between the sleeve and the cylinder head. Clean carefully and dry with compressed air and then dip the new 0-ring in a soap solution to facilitate assembly. Lubricate and fit the new nozzle sleeve with tool 884557. Knock in the sleeve until it reaches bottom.

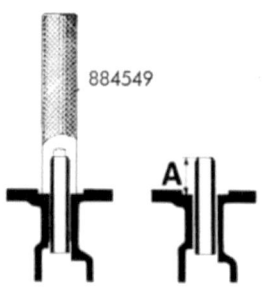

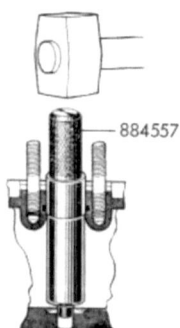

49. Lubricate the mandrel tool 884537 and insert the tool into the sleeve. (Ensure that the centre screw is sufficiently unscrewed.) Place some nuts or several washers on the studs so that the yoke can be tightened in place with the fixing nuts. Screw in the mandrel as far as the mating face of the sleeve allows. The mandrel is then withdrawn. Remove the tool.

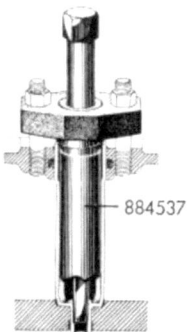

50. Adjust the length of sleeve protruding from the cylinder head face, (length is 0,9 mm) (0,0354 in.) and check that the sleeve is correctly fitted (dimension 19,5 mm). (0,7677 in.).

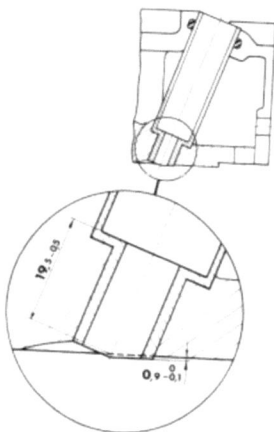

Valve and valve seat grinding

51. Machine the valve seats by milling or grinding them. Grind no more than is necessary to give the seat the correct shape and a good mating surface. The seat angle C shall be 45° and the width "B" approximately 1 mm (0,0394 in.). The width is adjusted with a 39° and a 60° miller respectively or a grinding disc. Clean the valves and grind them in a machine. The valves' face angle D shall be 44,5°. The sealing surface is ground no more than is necessary to "clean" it. If less than 1 mm (0,0394 in.) is left on the valve edge it is to be discarded. Likewise the valve is discarded if the valve stem is not straight or if dimension "A" exceeds 2,5 mm (0,0984 in.). Note! If this dimension is exceeded even if a new valve is fitted, the cylinder head must be changed.

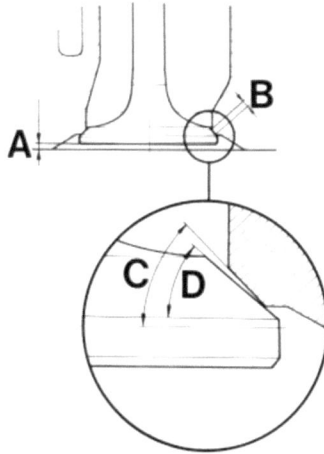

Rocker mechanism

52. Remove the circlip from the rocker shaft and remove the rocker arms. Clean the parts. Be particularly careful when cleaning the rocker shaft oil channels 3 and the rocker arm's oil hole, see also fig. 53.

53. Check the wear on the rocker shaft. Also check that the tappet adjustment screw's spherical part is neither deformed nor worn. The threads on the screw and the locknut must be undamaged.

Oval rocker arm bushes are to be replaced. Pressing in and out is performed with drift 884560. Press the bush in so that the oil hole assumes the position shown in the figure. The bush is reamed to a light push fit after it has been pressed in. Lubricate the shaft and assemble the rocker mechanism.

Pressure testing the nozzles
55. Check the shape of the jets at an opening pressure of 185 kp/cm^2 (2631 p.s.i.). Also check that the fuel spray discontinues simultaneously at all four holes and that no subsequent drops appear.

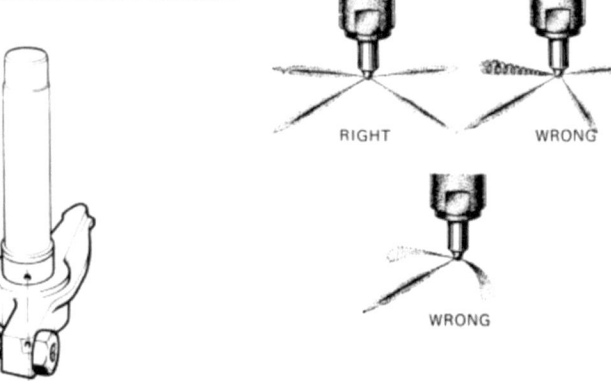

RIGHT WRONG

WRONG

54. Fit the rubber seal 1 on the inlet valve. Use tool 884497. Oil the valve sterns before they are inserted in their respective valve guides. Afterwards fit the valve springs, collars and collets with the help of a valve compressor.

Adjustment of opening pressure
56. The opening pressure is adjusted with adjustment washer 1, which is available in thicknesses between 1 mm (0.0394 in.) and 1,95 mm (0.0768 in.) with a difference of 0,05 (0,0020 in) mm between each size. Dismantle the nozzle and replace the washer with a thinner or thicker washer depending on whether the pressure is to be reduced or increased. Assemble the nozzle and check the opening pressure and jet shape. Continue until a satisfactory result is obtained.

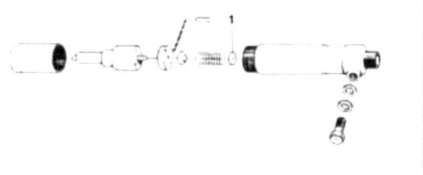

Flywheel cover and hand starting mechanism

57. Unscrew nut 1 and remove it and washer 2 holding the hand starting gearwheel 3. Then remove the gearwheel from the shaft A. Knock the shaft out from the cover. Loosen the set screw 5 which holds the spacer washer and knock out the spacer washer when the bearings 7 has been removed. Remove key 8, slide off the spacer ring 9 and pull off ball bearing 10 after which seal 11 can be pulled off. Note! If only the seal 11 is to be changed, pin 12 can be knocked out, after which the seal can be removed.

that the transmission cover must be machined since the new camshaft gear is thicker than the earlier gear and consequently there is not enough space for it in the transmission cover. The axial guide face distance A must be filed down by 3mm (0,1181 in.).

$15^{+0.5}_{+0.3}$ mm to $18^{+0.5}_{+0.3}$ mm (0.5906 $^{+0.0197}_{-0.0118}$ to 0.7087 $^{+0.0197}_{-0.0118}$ in.)

If the camshaft is damaged this means that the camshaft gear must be replaced in this case as well. This also means that the axial guide face must be filed down by 3 mm (0,1181 in.).

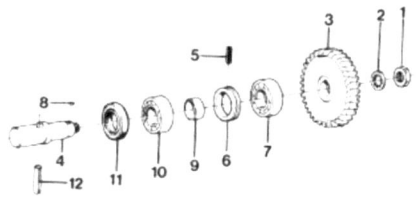

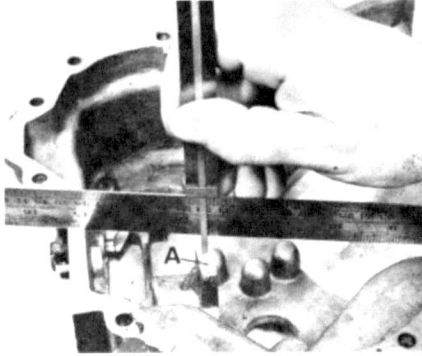

58. Replace damaged parts and reassemble the pin, seal, ball bearing and spacer ring on the shaft. Fit the spacer washer into the cover and tighten it in position with the set screw. Note! Ensure that the spacer washer's groove faces the locking screw's centre. Fit the shaft in the cover. Place the key in position and then the ball bearing. Fit the gearwheel. Secure it with a washer and nut. Knock out seal 1 from the flywheel cover. Press in a new seal afterwards.

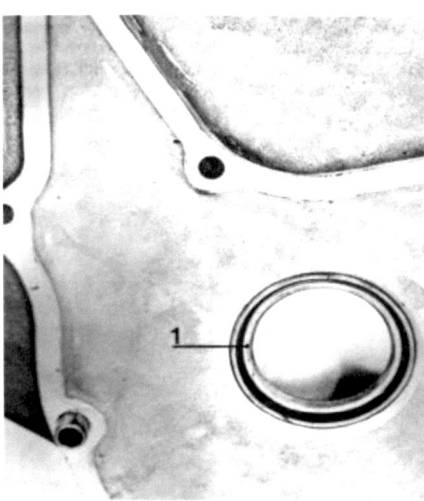

60. If the transmission cover is damaged and must be replaced, this means that even the camshaft and the camshaft gear must be replaced. The replacement is necessary because the axial guide in the new transmission cover is shortened by 3 mm (0,1181 in.) which in turn means that the camshaft will have an axial play of 3 mm (0,1181 in.).

The camshaft, camshaft gear and transmission cover are interchangable as of engine no. 1076 inclusive. When changing camshaft gears of a later type, the camshaft shall be pressed out of the camshaft gear.

Take care of the key. Check the camshaft for wear. See the technical data.

Place the key in the camshaft and press on the camshaft gear. The distance from the camshaft end to the camshaft gear's hub must be 136 mm (5,354 in.). See fig.

Camshaft

59. In such cases (on engines with engine nos. 100-1075) where a camshaft gear change is necessary, the camshaft must be changed as well. A new camshaft gear cannot be fitted to an early type of camshaft. Furthermore this means

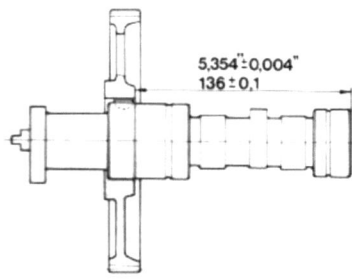

ASSEMBLING

61. Check that the liner is not scratched and that it is in good condition otherwise. Fit new O-rings 1 in the block (2 off) and a new O-ring 2 on the cylinder liner. Turn the mark on the liner (which was made during dismantling) to the mark on the block. Lubricate the O-rings and fit the liner. Be careful not to damage the O-rings.

63. Place the main bearing halves with the oil channel holes in the block. Then place the axial bearing halves in position. Turn the oil grooves 1 outwards.

62. When the cylinder liner is fitted in the block the height of the liner outside the block must be measured. The height must not exceed 0,05 mm (0,0020 in.) and must not be less than 0,01 mm (0,0004 in.), otherwise there is a risk that a leak can occur.

64. Oil both the bearing halves and place the crankshaft in position. Fit the main bearing shells in the bearing housings and place the axial bearings with the oil grooves outwards. Fit the bearing housing so that the indentation in the housing faces the same way as the indentation in the bearing half already in the block. Tighten the bearing housing with a torque of 70 Nm (7 kpm) (50 Lbft.).

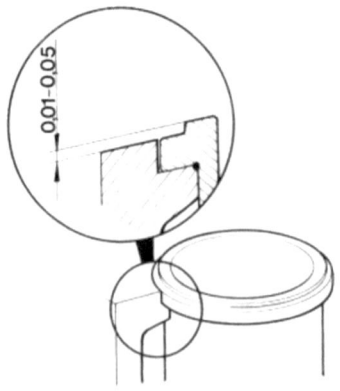

65. Remove any wear edges in the cylinder liner. Oil the cylinder liner and fit the piston in the block. Use a piston ring sleeve or tool 9992176. Turn the piston so that the machined depression in the piston crown faces the nozzle side.

67. Fit the camshaft with the camshaft gear. Align the marks on the crankshaft gear and the camshaft gear.

66. Oil and fit the big end bearing shells in the bearing half. Turn mark to the correct position and fit the bearing half. Tightening torque: 70 Nm (7 kpm) (50Lbft.).

68. Fit the governor. Tighten it in position with the set screw on the side. See that it goes into the groove.

69. Fit the gearwheel on the camshaft's opposite end.

71. Fit a new gasket for the transmission cover. Afterwards fit the transmission cover. Fix the lifting eye with the upper screw.

Adjustment of control rod travel
72. Fit a new gasket and fit the injector pump. Press on the ball end of the control arm. Measure and check that the control rod travel is correctly adjusted. (The same as prior to dismantling.) The measurement must be carried out with a new gasket. Set the control at full throttle. Press down the plunger to bottom position. Note that the cold start must not be engaged during measurement. The exact amount injected can only be determined when checking in a test bench.

70. Fit the oil pump. Note the different screw lengths.

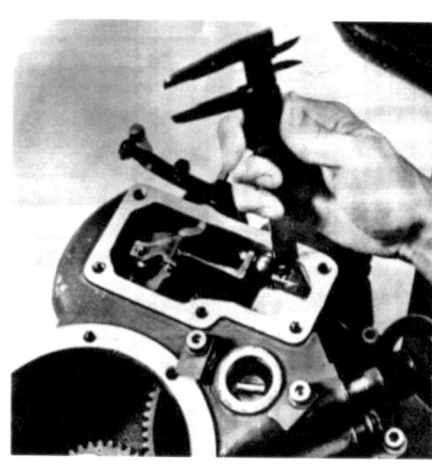

73. Release the plunger 8 mm (0,3150 in.) and measure the distance from the transmission cover face to the adjusting screw's contact point on the control arm.

75. If the engine smokes abnormally, the centre screw on the cover can be loosened and the adjusting screw can be adjusted until the engine runs smoke free. See the technical data for the correct injection amount.

74. Measure the adjusting screw's length and adjust any eventual deviation so that the plunger stops when released 8 mm. Screw down the cover afterwards.

76. Fit a new gasket and fit the flywheel cover. Be careful so that the sealing ring is not damaged. Trim the excessive gasket.

77. Fit a plane packing and then fit the sump. Note! On earlier engines a rubber seal was used. This is to be replaced by a plane packing.

79. Replace the tappet rods and fit the rocker mechanism. Check that the guide pin in the cylinder head goes into the hole in the rocker mechanism.

78. Lubricate and replace the valve lifters. Fit a new cylinder head gasket and then the cylinder head. Place the washers under the nuts and tighten the nuts in three stages to 70 Nm (7 kpm) (50Lbft.). See the tightening sequence.
First stage: 10 Nm (1 kpm) (7Lbft.).
Second stage: 40 Nm (4 kpm) (29Lbft.).
Third stage: 70 Nm (7 kpm) (50Lbft.).

80. Lubricate the oil filter rubber seal. Screw in the oil filter so far that the rubber seal first contacts the engine body. Afterwards screw in the filter a further half turn. Note! Tighten by hand. Then fit the feeder pump. Use a new O-ring between the pump and the engine.

81. Fit the fuel filter. Place sealing rings on both sides of the fuel pipe unions.

83. Connect the injector pipe, the temperature and oil pressure transmitters.

82. Fit the injector. The tightening torque = 10 Nm (1 kpm) (7Lbft.). Then connect the fuel drain pipe. Note! Place sealing rings on both sides of the pipe unions.

Thermostat testing
84. Lower the thermostat into hot water and check with a thermometer if the thermostat opens and closes correctly at the right temperature. It should start to open at $60^{0}C$ $140^{0}F$ and should be fully open at $90^{0}C$ $194^{0}F$. If the thermostat is defective it must be replaced. Clean the thermostat and fit a new gasket 1. Place the thermostat in the engine and fit the thermostat housing. Then fit the water pump and connect the coolant water hose.

85. Place the key for the gearbox connecting drive on the crankshaft on the gearbox side. Heat the connecting drive and fit it onto the crankshaft. Lock the drive with the large washer and the lockwasher. Tighten the screw with a torque wrench. The tightening torque is 70 Nm (7 kpm) (50Lbft.). Use a counter force. Bend the lockwasher up against the screw head afterwards.

87. Fit the starter motor and the alternator. Note! Place the spacer tube correctly and assemble the belt tensioner. Fit and tension the drive belt so that it can be depressed 3—4 mm (0,1181—0,1575 in) with normal thumb pressure.

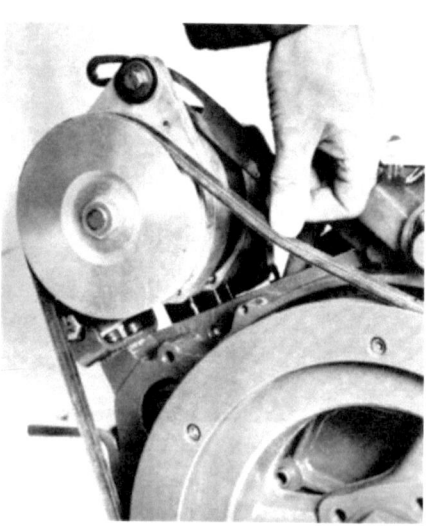

86. Place the key for the flywheel in the crankshaft's key slot. Fit and tighten the flywheel. Use a counter force in the spokes of the flywheel. The tightening torque is 500 Nm (50 kpm) (362Lbft.). Spanner jaw width is 55 mm (2 5/32").

Tappet adjustment
88. Turn the flywheel until both tappets function. Turn the flywheel a further complete turn and adjust the tappets. The clearance is 0,30 mm (0,0118 in.) for the inlet valve (nearest flywheel) and 0,35 mm 10,0138 in.) for the exhaust valve when the engine is hot. Fit the rocker box cover and a new gasket.

INJECTION ANGLE CONTROL
89. A Wilbär tube is used when checking the injection angle. Fit the Wilbär tube on the pressure pipe nipple.

91. Open the level valve 1 on the measuring apparatus so that the level lies 25 - 30 mm (1" - 2 3/16") from the bottom. Turn the engine in the rotation direction until compression is felt.

90. Rotate the engine in the correct direction until the level tube 1 is full with air-free fuel.

92. If the injection angle does not meet the prescribed value, the number of washers 1 between the pump housing and the transmission cover is increased or decreased until the correct value is obtained. One washer gives a difference in injection angle of approximately 1°.

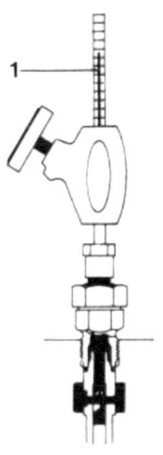

93. Fit the exhaust elbow and the gearbox. Use new gaskets. Check that the rubber damper is not damaged.

BLEEDING THE FUEL SYSTEM

94. Fuel system bleeding is always carried out in the following cases: When the microfilter is changed - when draining via the drain plug - when cleaning the gauze in the fuel pump - when the fuel tank has run dry - when fitting an injector pump - after leaks in or repairs on, the fuel piping - when the engine has been out of use for a long time.
Bleeding is carried out as follows:
Open the air bleed screw 1 in the microfilter. Pump up fuel using the hand pump 2 until clean air-free fuel runs out. Close the air bleed screw. If the pump effect is poor rotate the engine until the pump's drive cam assumes another position. If the injector pump has been dismantled or, when the engine is to be started for the first time after renovation, the injection pump must be bled. Open the air bleed screw 3 on the injection pump. Pump the hand pump 2 until air-free fuel runs out. Loosen the pressure connection 4 and rotate the engine with the starter motor until fuel runs out from the pressure pipe. Tighten the pressure connection and start the engine.

ELECTRICAL SYSTEM

IMPORTANT

The following applies to engines fitted with alternators:

1. **Do not break the electrical circuit between the alternator and the battery when the engine is running. If a main switch is fitted it must therefore not be turned off until the engine is stopped.**
   No lead must be disconnected when the engine is running since this can irreparably damage the charging regulator.

2. The battery, battery cable and cable terminals are to be checked regularly. The battery poles are to be properly clean and the cable terminals are to be tight and well greased so that a break in the circuit cannot occur. All other cables are to be properly connected, no loose connections must occur. The battery's positive and negative connections must on no condition be exchanged when the battery is connected.

3. When starting with an auxiliary battery, check first that it has the same rated voltage as the standard battery. Connect the auxiliary battery with positive to positive and negative to negative. Remove the auxiliary battery when the engine has started. Note! The cables to the standard battery must on no condition be disconnected.

4. When carrying out electrical welding on the engine or associated installation parts the charging regulator's cable must be disconnected and insulated first. Afterwards both the battery cable terminals can be removed.

5. When carrying out repairs on the generator, both battery cable terminals must always be disconnected. The same applies if the battery is given a quick charge.

6. Never test a connection with a screwdriver or similar tool to see if it sparks.

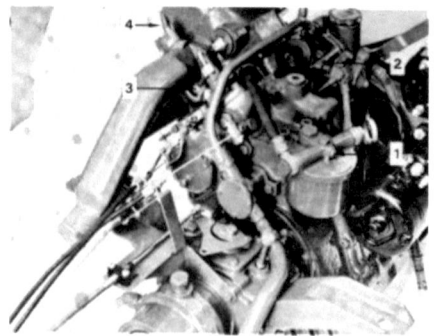

Wiring Diagram
Cable Marking

Designation	Colour	mm²	A.W.G.
A	White	6	9
B	Black	1.5	15
B'	Black	0.6	19
B"	Black	0.75	18
C	Red	6	9
C'	Red	35	1
C"	Red	0.6	19
F	Yellow	1.5	15
G	Brown	1.5	15
H'	Blue	35	1
I	Green/Red	1.5	15
I'	Green/Red	0.75	18
J	Green	1.5	15
J'	Green	0.6	19
J"	Green	0.75	18
K	Blue/Yellow	0.75	18
L	White/Red	0.75	18
M	Blue/Red	0.75	18

Circuit explanation

1. Extra switch
2. Charging control lamp
3. Temperature warning lamp
4. Oil pressure warning lamp
5. Key switch
6. Warning unit
7. Screw
8. Charging control lamp (for secondary battery circuit, extra equipment)
9. Place for instruments, extra equipment.
10. Snap connection
11. Starter motor
12. Alternator
13. Fusebox
14. Main switch
15. Battery
16. Temperature sender
17. Oil pressure sender

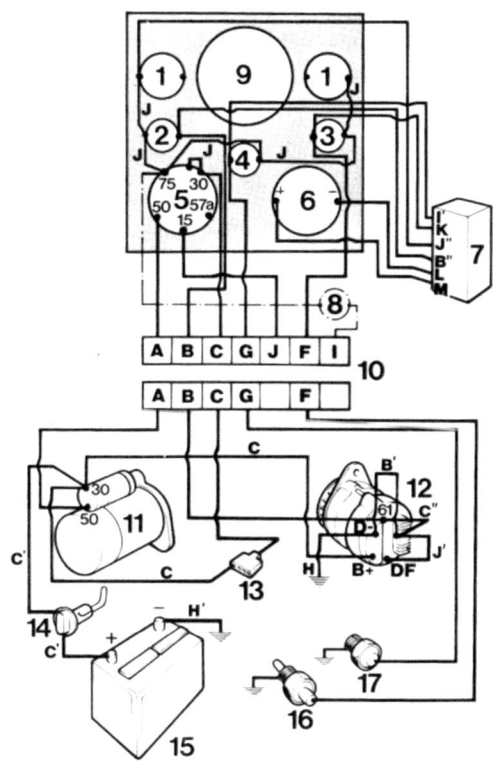

27

FAULT TRACING

The fault finding chart given below only covers the most common faults which occur.

Engine will not start	Engine stops	The engine does not reach the correct speed at full throttle	The engine runs rough or vibrates abnormally	The engine becomes abnormally hot	FAULT	Note
X					Main switch not connected, flat battery, cable disconnected.	See para A
X	X				Empty fuel tank, fuel tap closed, blocked fuel filter.	See para B
X	X		X		Water, air or impurities in the fuel.	See para B
X	X	X	X		Faulty injector.	See para C
	X				Boat abnormally loaded, boat bilge fouled with weedgrowth.	See para C
		X	X		Propeller damaged.	See para E
				X	Clogged coolant water intake, cooling vanes, defective pump wheel or thermostat.	See para F

A. Check the charge state of the battery with the help of a hydrometer which shows the specific gravity of the battery acid. This varies according to the state of the charge, (see the technical data). (See furthermore "Electrical system" p. 26.)

B. Change the microfilter by unscrewing the hexagonal head on the filter holder's base. The microfilter and its holder are of a discardable type which means that the old filter is discarded and a new one fitted. Check that the face of the cover is completely clean and that the filter packing is undamaged. Screw the new filter by hand until the packing contacts the cover. Then tighten the filter a further half turn. There is a drain plug in the bottom of the filter holder for draining water and impurities in the fuel. Bleed the fuel system after draining and after a filter change and then check for tightness.
Remove the cover on the feed pump and clean the prefilter in diesel oil. Refit the filter with the notches upward and fit an undamaged packing and tighten the cover. Bleed the fuel system.
Check and drain when necessary the extra fuel filter if one is fitted. Look out for spilled fuel.

C. Check the injector with reference to opening pressure, tightness and jet shape. It is recommended that these checks be carried out after a maximum operation time of 400 hours or once per season. See also paragraphs 55 and 56.

D. To obtain the best operational economy, the engine speed should be at least 300 r.p.m. less that the maximum obtainable during extended running periods. Note! If the boat has been in the water a considerable time, the maximum obtainable engine speed can decrease due to growth on the hull's underside. Use growth inhibiting bottom paint.
Check and clean the hull regularly.

E. Check that the propeller blades are whole. If any of the propeller blades are damaged, the propeller should be changed. A propeller blade can be out of line (twisted) – this is very difficult to detect. Place the propeller on a flat surface and measure the blades. If any blade is twisted the propeller should be changed.

F. Check the coolant system from the point of view of leakage, blockage etc.
Check that the thermostat opens at the correct temperature. The thermostat can be taken out when the thermostat housing has been dismantled. See also paragraph 84.
The pump impeller in the sea water pump is made of neoprene rubber and can be damaged when the water supply is cut off, for instance if there is a blockage in the sea water intake. Paragraphs 23—27 should be followed when changing a pump impeller and sealing rings. Note) If the boat is in the water the sea cock must be closed before the sea water is dismantled. Do not forget to open the cock again.

Special tools for the MD5A

Part No	Designation
884538	Drift for pressing out valve guides
884549	Drift for pressing in valve guides
884557	Drift for pressing in injector sleeve.
884541	Tool for removing injector sleeve.
884537	Drift for copper sleeve.
884551 + 884231 (screw and nut from MD21-MD32)	Tool for removing cylinder liner.
884560	Drift for removing rocker arm bush.
884497	Drift for fitting rubber valve seal.
884543	Nipple fixture
884535	Nipple for compression pressure measurement.

TECHNICAL DATA

General
Type designation | MD5A
Effect (DIN) at 40 r/s (2500 r.p.m.) | 5.5 kW | (7.5 b.h.p)
No. of cylinders | 1
Bore | 84 mm | (3.31 in.)
Stroke | 80 mm | (3.15 in.)
Displacement, total | 0,443 dm^3 | (27 cu. in.)
Compression ratio | 16,5:1
Compression pressure at starter motor speed | 20 - 22 kp/cm^2 11 | (144 - 159 psi)
Direction rotation, viewed from flywheel | Clockwise
Idling speed | 9,2 - 10,8 r/s | (550 - 650 r/m)

Cylinders
Cylinder liner, wet replaceable
Cylinder diameter, standard mm (in.) | 84,000 - 84,015 | (3.3071 - 3.3077)

Pistons
Overall height mm (in.) | 77 (3,0315)
Height from gudgeon pin centre to piston crown mm (in.) | 49,0 - 49,05 | (1.9291 - 1.9311)
Piston clearance mm (in.) | 0,081 - 0,114 | (0.0032 - 0.0045)
Pistons available as standard mm (in.) | 83,901 - 83,919 | (3.3032 - 3.3039)

Gudgeon pins
Diameter mm (in.) | 25,996 - 26,000 | (1.0235 - 1.0236)
Inner diameter of gudgeon pin bush mm (in.) | 25,999 - 26,004 | (1.0236 - 1.0237)
Clearance between gudgeon pin and bush mm (in.) | 0,001 - 0,008 | (0.00004 - 0.0003)

Piston rings
Number of compression rings | 2
Number of oil rings | 1
The upper compression ring has a chromium insert

Axial piston ring clearance
Upper compression ring mm (in.) | 0,070 - 0,102 | (0.0028 - 0.0040)
Lower compression ring mm (in.) | 0,050 - 0,082 | (0.0020 - 0.0032)
Oil scraper ring mm (in.) | 0,030 - 0,062 | (0.0012 - 0.0024)

Piston ring gap in cylinder
Upper compression ring mm (in.) | 0,30 - 0,50 | (0.0118 - 0.0197)
Lower compression ring mm (in.) | 0,30 - 0,50 | (0.0118 - 0.0197)
Oil scraper ring mm (in.) | 0,25 - 0,50 | (0.0098 - 0.0197)

Crankshaft
Axial clearance (end float) mm (in.) | 0,05 - 0,30 | (0.0020 - 0.0118)
Main bearings radial clearance mm (in.) | 0,040 - 0,096 | (0.0016 - 0.0038)
Big end bearing radial clearance mm (in.) | 0,040 - 0,096 | (0.0016 - 0.0038)

Main bearing journals
Diameter, standard mm (in.) | 53,987 - 54,000 | (2.1255 - 2.1260)
Diameter, undersized, 0,250 mm (in.) | 53,737 - 53,750 | (2.1156 - 2.1161)
Diameter, undersized, 0,500 mm (in.) | 53,487 - 53,500 | (2.1058 - 2.1063)

Main bearing shells
Thickness, standard mm (in.) | 1,968 - 1,980 | (0.0775 - 0.0780)
Oversized, 0,250 mm (in.) | 2,093 - 2,105 | (0.0824 - 0.0829)
Oversized, 0,500 mm (in.) | 2,218 - 2,230 | (0.0873 - 0.0878)

1) Measured with a Moto Meter, nipple 884535 and fixture 884543.

Connecting rod journals
Diameter, standard mm (in.)	50,987 - 51,000	(2.0074 - 2.0079)
Diameter, undersized, 0,250 mm (in.)	50,737 - 50,750	(1.9975 - 1.9980)
Diameter, undersized, 0,500 mm (in.)	50,487 - 50,500	(1.9877 - 1.9882)

Big end bearing shells
Thickness, standard mm (in.)	1,768 - 1,780	(0.0696 - 0.0701)
Oversized, 0,250 mm (in.)	1,893 - 1,905	(0.0745 - 0.0750)
Oversized, 0,500 mm (in.)	2,018 - 2,030	(0.0794 - 0.0799)

Connecting rod
Axial clearance (end float) at crankshaft mm (in.)	0,05 - 0,20	(0.0020 - 0.0079)

Camshaft
Axial clearance (end float) mm (in.)	0,54 - 0,82	(0.0213 - 0.0323)
Radial clearance in bearings mm (in.)	0,025 - 0,075	(0.0010 - 0.0030)
Camshaft diameter mm (in.)	39,975 - 40,000	(1.5738 - 1.5748)
Camshaft diameter mm (in.)	46,975 - 47,000	(1.8494 - 1.8504)
Lifting height mm (in.)	5,8	(0,2283)
Bearing diameter mm (in.)	40,025 - 40,050	(1.5758 - 1.5768)
Bearing diameter mm (in.)	47,025 - 47,050	(1.8514 - 1.8524)

Inlet valve
Valve disc diameter mm (in.)	34,9 - 35,1	(1.3740 - 1.3819)
Valve stem diameter mm (in.)	7,955 - 7,970	(0.3132 - 0.3138)
Valve seat angle	45,5°	(see fig. page 15)
Seat angle in cylinder head	45°	
Seat width in cylinder. head mm (in.)	ca 1	(0.0394)
Tappet clearance, hot mm (in.)	0,30	(0.0118)

Outlet valve
Valve disc diameter mm (in.)	27,9 - 28,1	(1.0984 - 1.1063)
Valve stem diameter mm (in.)	7,925 - 7,940	(0.3120 - 0.3126)
Valve seat angle	44,5°	(see fig. page 15)
Seat angle in cylinder head	45°	
Seat width in cylinder head mm (in.)	ca 1	(0.0394)
Tappet clearance, hot mm (in.)	0,35	(0.0138)

Valve guides
Length, inlet valve mm (in.)	52	(2.0472)
Length, exhaust valve mm (in.)	52	(2.0472)
Inner diameter mm (in.)	8,000 - 8,015	(0.3150 - 0.3156)
Height above cylinder block's spring face mm (in.)	10,65 - 11,35	(0.4193 - 0.4469)
Clearance, valve stem-valve guide: inlet valve mm (in.)	0,030 - 0,060	(0.0012 - 0.0024)
Clearance, valve stem-valve guide: outlet valve mm (in.)	0,060 - 0,090	(0.0024 - 0.0035)

Valve springs
Length unloaded mm (ln.)	42,5	(1.6732)
Loaded with a force of 170 N (17 kp) (37,5 lb) mm (in.)	32	(1.2598)
Loaded with a force of 300 N (30 kp) (66 lb) mm (in.)	24	(0.9449)

Lubrication system
Engine oil capacity ex. filter (Imp. qts. = US qts.)	2,0 din^3	(1.7 = 2.1)
Engine oil capacity inc. filter (Imp. qts. = US qts.)	2,1 din^3	(1.8 = 2.2)
Oil quality according to API system	CD	(DS)
1st alternative. Above + 10^{0}C (5Q0 F) Volvo Penta oil Double grade	SAE 20W/30	
Below + 10^{0}C (50^{0}F) Volvo Penta oil Single grade	SAE l0W	
2nd alternative. Viscosity above + 10^{0}Cj50^{0}F)	SAE 20	
Viscosity below + 100 (50~ F)	SAE 10	
Oil pressure, hot engine, idling kplcm^2 (p.s.i.)	1,5 - 2,5 kplcm^2	(21 - 36)
Oil pressure, hot engine, full throttle kplcm^2 (p.s.i.)	4,0 - 5,0 kplcm^2	(57 - 71)

Lubrication oil filter
Designation MANN W 77 or FRAM PH3614

Lubrication oil pump
Type Gear pump
Spring for pressure reduction valve: Length unloaded mm (in.)
    40 (1.5748)
Loaded with 25 N (2,5 kp) (5,5 lb) mm (in.). .   34 (1.3386)
Loaded with 35 N (3,5 kp) (7,7 lb) mm (in.) .   31,5 (1.2402)
Gear's axial clearance including packing mm (in.)   0,010 - 0,130 (0.0004—0.0051)

Fuel system
Injector pump, Bosch PFR 1K 70A 431/11
Injector, Bosch, holder KBAL 65
Nozzle DLLA 150
Hole diameter mm (in.) Four, 0,23 (0.0091)
Opening pressure (new nozzle) kp/cm^2 (p.s.i.) 185 (2631)
Nozzle angle 150°
Pre-injection angle 25 - 28°
Fuel quantity injected 31 min^3/stroke at 33,3 r/s (2000 r.p.m)

Micro Filter
Type Bosch 0 450 015 003
Filter element Bosch 1 457 431 324

Feed pump
Type Pierburg PE 15672
Feed pressure at 42 r/s (2500 r.p.in) kp/cm^2 (p.s.i) 0,65 - 0,85 (9.2 - 12.1)

Electrical system
Battery voltage 12 V
Battery capacity Max. 60 Ah
Alternator rating, max 35 A
Starter motor rating 0,81 kW (1.1 hp)
Battery electrolyte spec. gray: Fully charged battery 1,275 - 1,285 g/cm^3
Charging to be carried out at 1,230 g/cm^3

Cooling system
Thermostat Bellows thermostat
Starts to open at ^{0}C (^{0}F) 60 (140)
Fully open at ^{0}C (^{0}F) 90 (194)

WEAR TOLERANCES
Cylinders (liner)
Replaced when worn (or if the engine has an abnormally high oil consumption) mm (in.)   0,25 (0.0098)

Crankshaft
Main and big end bearings
Permissible ovality mm (in.) 0,06 (0.0024)
Permissible conicity mm (in.) 0,05 (0.0020)
Max. axial clearance (end float) mm (in.) 0,36 (0.0142)

Camshaft
Bearing journals, permissible ovality tom (in.) 0,03 (0.0012)
Max. clearance between camshaft and bearings mm (in.) 0,15 (0.0059)

Valves
Max. clearance between valve guide and valve stem mm (in.) 0,16 (0.0063)
Valve disc edge mm. thickness mm (in.) 1,0 (0.0394)

TIGHTENING TORQUES

Cylinder head nuts*	70 Nm	(7 kpm)	(50Lbft.)
Cylinder head studs	20 Nm	(2 kpm)	(14Lbft.)
Screw for a gearbox drive on crankshaft	80 Nm	(8 kpm)	(58 Lbft.)
Flywheel nut	500 Nm	(50 kpm)	(362Lbft.)
Big end (connecting rod) bearings	70 Nm	(7 kpm)	(50Lbft.)
Water pump drive	60 Nm	(6 kpm)	(43Lbft.)
Main bearings	70 Nm	(7 kpm)	(50 Lbtt.)
Nuts for injector holder	10 Nm	(1 kpm)	(7Lbft.)

Tightening torque for cylinder head nuts.

* Note! The tightening must be done in three stages.
First stage: 10 Nm (1 kpm) (7Lbft.)
Second stage: 40 Nm (4 kpm) (29Lbft.)
Final stage: 70 Nm (7 kpm) (50Lbft.)

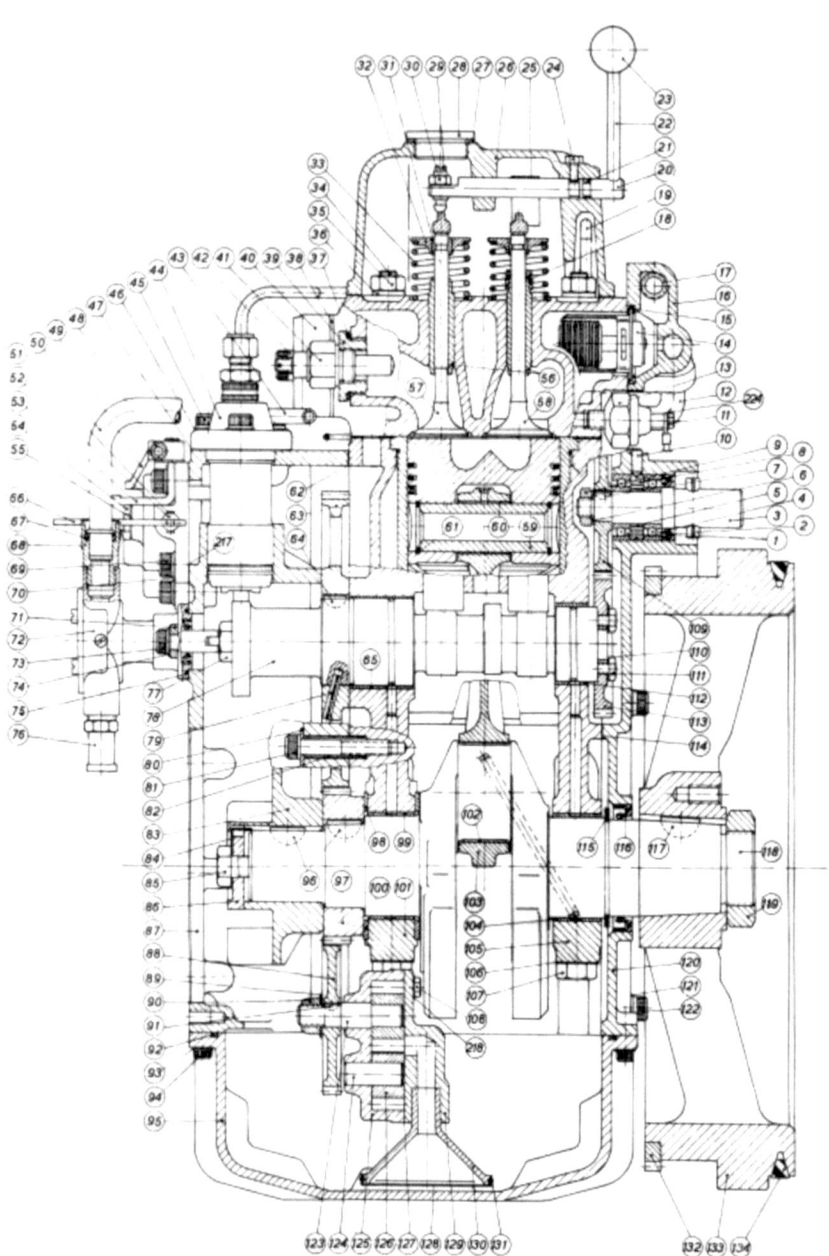

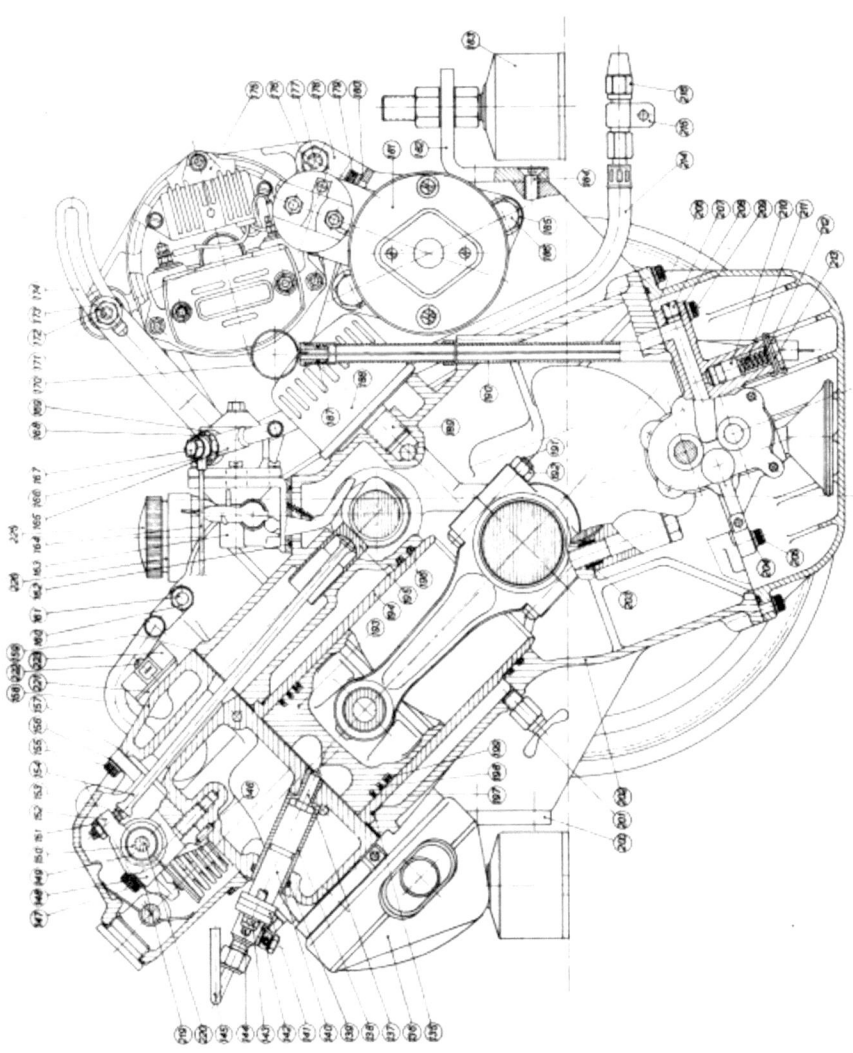